Joan Elliott's
CROSS STITCH GREETING
CARDS

70 stunning designs for everv occasion

D&C
David and Charles

For Cheryl with my love, thanks
and fondest admiration.

A DAVID & CHARLES BOOK
Copyright © David & Charles Limited 2010

David & Charles is an F+W Media Inc. company
4700 East Galbraith Road
Cincinnati, OH 45236

First published in the UK and US in 2010
Reprinted in 2010

Text and designs copyright © Joan Elliott 2010
Layout and photography copyright © David & Charles 2010

A catalogue record for this book is available from the
British Library.

ISBN-13: 978-0-7153-3289-4 paperback
ISBN-10: 0-7153-3289-9 paperback

Printed in China by RR Donnelley
for David & Charles
Brunel House   Newton Abbot   Devon

Commissioning Editor Cheryl Brown
Assistant Editor Nikki Van Staden
Project Editor and Chart Preparation Lin Clements
Art Editor Sarah Clark
Designer Victoria Marks
Photography Kim Sayer and Karl Adamson
Production Controller Kelly Smith

David and Charles publish high quality books on a wide
range of subjects. For more great book ideas visit:
www.rucraft.co.uk

Contents

Introduction

Greetings everyone, and welcome to my new collection of cross stitch cards. In this world of fast-moving emails and instant messaging, how wonderful it is to slow down and spend time working on something that is hand-made, adding your own special touch and creativity to a true gift from the heart.

In this book there are designs for every occasion, making a special day even more memorable for whomever is lucky enough to receive one of your cards. The designs are suitable for a wide range of friends and relatives, celebrating all the important people and events in our lives and you will be spoilt for choice when you see the beautiful collections of cards in each of the eight chapters.

Everything you need to know about stitching the designs is given in Stitching Advice overleaf, while making and finishing cards attractively is described on pages 12–15. The card designs are very versatile and many of the chapters give simple ideas for making the designs up as gifts. The designs can also be personalized using the alphabets on pages 108–109. So then, there is no better way to finish this introduction than for me to wish all of you 'Happy Everything'...

and many hours of 'Happy Stitching'!

Joan

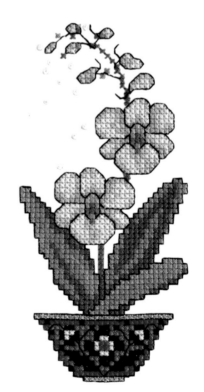

Eastern Promise brings the calming spirit and beauty of design that is inherent in Asian art. From dancing koi to a splendid birthday kimono, the designs have just the right dash of elegance.

Celtic Celebrations has a collection of stylish designs filled with Celtic spirit and features an array of knotwork patterns, beautiful arts and crafts flowers and fabulous mythical beasts.

Sampler Sentiments allows you to create charming heirlooms for a variety of personal milestones. Their special antique quality makes many of the cards suitable for framing as miniature pictures.

Say It With Flowers will appeal to all passionate gardeners. I created these lovely floral designs with favourites from the garden, including bluebells, poppies, primroses and clover.

Nearest and Dearest honours those closest to you with light-hearted designs sure to bring a smile. Be it a birthday, a job well done, or to say 'I love you', families always find cause for celebration.

Welcome Baby has fabulous cards to welcome a newborn into the fold. Teddies and ducklings, baby rattles and balloons all combine to rejoice in the happy event.

Childhood Fun is filled with colourful cards celebrating your little one's childhood and there are plenty of reasons to stitch up some of the great cards from this chapter.

Happy Everything celebrates all those annual events that bring us such joy. From Valentine's Day to Christmas, all year long these fun cards will keep you stitching.

Stitching Advice

This section describes the materials and equipment required, the basic techniques and stitches used and some general making up methods. Refer to Suppliers for useful addresses.

Materials

Fabrics

The designs have been worked mostly on a blockweave fabric called Aida, predominantly on a 14-count size, which is very easy to stitch on. If you change the gauge (count) of the material, that is the number of holes per inch, then the size of the finished work will alter accordingly. Some of the designs have been stitched on evenweave and in this case need to be worked over two fabric threads instead of one block.

Some designs use a hand-dyed fabric from Polstitches (see Suppliers for contact details), which adds an extra dimension, but you could use a solid pastel instead if you prefer.

Threads

The designs have been stitched with DMC stranded embroidery cotton (floss) but you could match the colours to other thread ranges – ask at your local needlework store. The six-stranded skeins can easily be split into separate strands. The card instructions tell you how many strands to use.

DMC Color Variations threads have been used for some designs: these are variegated colours and are used in the same way as stranded cotton.

DMC Satin floss threads have also been used in some cards. These threads have a soft, satin sheen that accents different areas of a design.

Some of the cards use Kreinik #4 Very Fine braid, a metallic thread that adds an attractive glitter – use one strand when working with this thread.

Needles

Tapestry needles, available in different sizes, are used for cross stitch as they have a rounded point and do not snag fabric. You will need a thinner beading needle to attach the small glass seed beads used in some of the cards.

Frames

It is a matter of personal preference as to whether you use an embroidery frame to keep your fabric taut while stitching. Generally speaking, working with a frame helps to keep the tension even and prevent distortion, while working without a frame is faster and less cumbersome. There are various types on the market – look in your local needlework store for examples.

Beads

Some of the card designs feature glass seed beads, which bring an extra dimension to the cross stitch and make the greeting card just that extra bit special. Mill Hill glass seed beads have been used but you could substitute other seed beads.

Techniques

Preparing the Fabric

Before starting work, check the design size given with each project and make sure that this is the size you require for your finished embroidery. Your fabric should be at least 5cm (2in) larger all the way round than the finished size of the stitching, to allow for making up. Before beginning to stitch, neaten the fabric edges either by hemming or zigzagging to prevent fraying as you work.

Finding the Fabric Centre

Marking the centre of the fabric is important regardless of which direction you work from, in order to stitch the design centrally on the fabric. To find the centre, fold the fabric in half horizontally and then vertically, then tack (baste) along the folds (or use tailor's chalk). The centre point is where the two lines of tacking (basting) meet. This point on the fabric should correspond to the centre point on the chart. Remove these lines on completion of the work.

Calculating Design Size

Each project gives the stitch count, which is the number of stitches across the height and width of a design, and the finished design size, which is the size the design will be once stitching is complete. The finished size will depend on the fabric size or count you are using. If you want to work the design on fabric with a different count you will need to re-calculate the finished size.To do this, count the number of stitches in each direction on the chart and divide these numbers by the fabric count number, e.g., 140 x 140 ÷ 14-count = a design size of 10 x 10in (25.5 x 25.5cm). Working on evenweave usually means working over two fabric threads, so divide the fabric count by two before you start calculating.

Using Charts and Keys

The charts in this book are easy to work from. Each square represents one stitch. Each coloured square, or coloured square with a symbol, represents a thread colour, with the code number given in the chart key. Some designs use fractional stitches (three-quarter cross stitches) to give more definition. Solid coloured lines show where backstitches or long stitches are to be worked. French knots are shown by coloured circles. Larger coloured circles with a dot indicate beads. Each complete chart has arrows at the side to show the centre point, which you could mark with a pen.

37 stitches wide

37 stitches high

Twice as Nice
DMC stranded cotton

Cross stitch (2 strands)			Backstitch (1 strand)	French knots (2 strands)
■ 553	✕ 729	✓ 964	— 553	● 553
603	869	Color Variations 4050	— 603	● 938
v 605	■ 938		— 938	
676	959			

Starting and Finishing Stitching

Avoid using knots when starting and finishing as this will make your work uneven and lumpy when mounted. Instead, bring the needle up at the start of the first stitch, leaving a 'tail' of about 2.5cm (1in) at the back. Secure this tail by working the first few stitches over it. Start new threads by first passing the needle through several stitches on the back of the work.

To finish off thread, pass the needle through several nearby stitches on the wrong side of the work, then cut the thread off close to the fabric.

Washing and Pressing

If you need to wash your finished embroidery, first make sure the stranded cottons are colourfast by washing them in tepid water and mild soap. Rinse well and lay out flat to dry completely before stitching. Wash completed embroideries in the same way. To iron embroidery, use a medium setting, covering the ironing board with a thick layer of towelling. Place the stitching right side down and press gently, taking care with glass seed beads and metallic threads.

Starting and finishing neatly will make your cross stitch look its best when mounted in a card

Stitches

Backstitch

Backstitches are used to give definition to parts of a design and to outline areas. Many of the charts use different coloured backstitches. Follow Fig 1 below, bringing the needle up at 1, down at 2, up again at 3, down at 4 and so on.

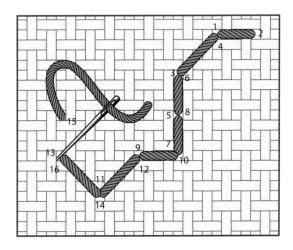

Fig 1 Working backstitch

Cross Stitch

A cross stitch can be worked singly (Fig 2a) or half stitches can be sewn in a line and completed on the return journey (Fig 2b).

To make a cross stitch over one block of Aida, bring the needle up through the fabric at the bottom left side of the stitch (number 1 on Fig 2a) and cross diagonally to the top right corner (number 2). Push the needle through the hole and bring up through at 3, crossing the fabric diagonally to finish the stitch at 4. To work the next stitch, come up through the bottom right corner of the first stitch and repeat the sequence.

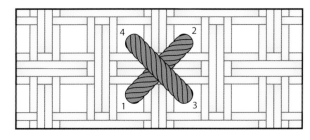

Fig 2a Working a single cross stitch on Aida fabric

To work a line of cross stitches, stitch the first part of the stitch as above and repeat these half cross stitches along the row. Complete the crosses on the way back. Note: for neat work, always finish the cross stitch with the top stitches lying in the same diagonal direction.

Fig 2b Working cross stitch in two journeys

French Knot

French knots have been used for details in some of the designs. To work, follow Fig 3, bringing the needle and thread up through the fabric at the exact place where the knot is to be positioned. Wrap the thread once or twice around the needle (according to the project instructions), holding the thread firmly close to the needle, then twist the needle back through the fabric close to where it first emerged. Holding the knot down, pull the thread through carefully to the back leaving the knot on the surface, securing it with one small stitch on the back.

Fig 3 Working a French knot

Long Stitch

This stitch is used in some of the projects. Simply work a long, straight stitch (Fig 4) starting and finishing at the points indicated on the chart.

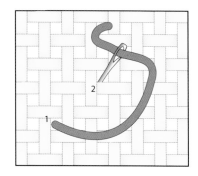

Fig 4 Working a long stitch

Three-quarter Cross Stitch

Three-quarter cross stitches give more detail to a design and can create the illusion of curves. They are shown by a triangle within a square on the charts. These stitches are easier on evenweave fabric than Aida (see Fig 5). To work on Aida, make a half cross stitch from corner to corner of the Aida square and then work a quarter cross stitch across the other diagonal, piercing the Aida square and anchoring the half stitch.

Fig 5 Working three-quarter cross stitch on evenweave

Attaching Beads

Adding beads will bring sparkle and texture to your cross stitch embroidery. Attach seed beads using ordinary sewing thread that matches the fabric colour and a beading needle or very fine 'sharp' needle and a half or whole cross stitch (Fig 6).

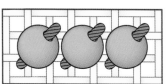

Fig 6 Attaching beads

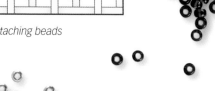

Card Making and Finishing

The designs in this book are sized for making up lovely cards and this section shows you how to make single-fold and double-fold cards and how to mount your embroidery on to them. Making up a card is easy and can be done with either ready-made card mounts or by fashioning your own unique cards. Card making and scrapbooking are very popular crafts so there are many card sizes, colours, paper textures and aperture shapes available (see some suppliers on page 110). You'll have great fun exploring the shelves of your local stationery and craft shops too.

Whether using ready-mades or your own home-made cards, measure each design to determine how large an aperture you will need, adding an extra three rows all around to border the design. Designs can also be mounted on blank single-fold cards without apertures giving a light-hearted, more casual feel that suits many of the whimsical designs nicely.

This section also gives advice on finishing off your cards beautifully, showing how trims and embellishments used can give an extra special, personalized look.

Customizing Cards

Additional alphabets and numbers are charted on pages 108–109, which will allow you to add names, dates and other messages to your cards. You could allow a little extra fabric at the top or bottom of a design to provide space for words. Plan the names or messages on graph paper first to ensure they fit the space you have allowed.

Using Iron-on Interfacing

Before you mount work in cards it is helpful to back your finished embroidery with iron-on interfacing. This will stiffen the fabric and help to prevent the edges from fraying, especially when using evenweave fabrics.

Cut a piece of iron-on interfacing about 2.5cm (1in) larger than the design all around and fuse it to the back of the embroidery according to the manufacturer's instructions and then trim the fabric to the size required. Using this extra step is also helpful when mounting light-coloured fabrics on dark-coloured cards to prevent the darker colour showing through to the embroidery.

Making a Single-Fold Card

A single-fold card without an aperture is the easiest type of card to make and the embroidery is generally attached to the card front with glue or double-sided tape. You could also experiment with adding various mounts in different shapes and sizes to the card front – see the box below. You will need: thick cardstock (between 160–240gsm) in a colour of your choice; cutting mat; craft knife; metal ruler and bone folder (optional).

1 Decide what size the front of the card needs to be and then cut a piece of thick card to twice that width.

2 Fold the card in half, using a bone folder or the back of a blunt knife to make a sharp crease.

Using Mounts

Adding an extra mount or two can help to display your cross stitch. Try using plain card to tone or contrast with the design, or use one of the many decorative papers that are available. Try rotating the mount or positioning it in different places on the card front to see which effect you like best. A double mount can look very attractive.

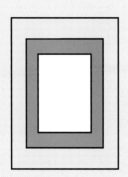
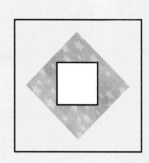

Mounting Embroidery on a Single-Fold Card

Many of the embroideries made for single-fold cards look nice with a frayed edge, as the Birthday Kimono card shown here. Alternatively, the edges could be covered with a decorative trim once the embroidery is stuck to the card front.

1 Back the embroidery with iron-on interfacing as described above and trim it to the size required, checking that it will fit on the front of the card. If you want a fringed edge, iron on a slightly smaller piece of interfacing to allow some fabric to be frayed before the card is mounted.

2 Apply strips of double-sided adhesive tape to the back of the embroidery and stick it on the card front in the position you've decided upon. This may be centrally placed or offset to either the top or bottom of the card – see box overleaf for advice.

Positioning the Embroidery

The simplest cross stitch embroidery can take on a new dimension depending on its position on the card front, so experiment with some layouts, as shown here.

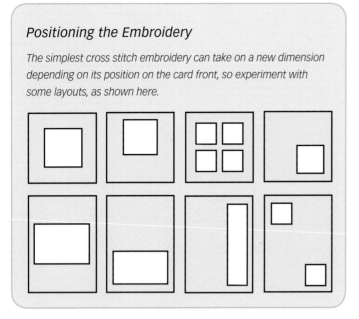

3 You can now embellish your card as desired. There are thousands of trims and toppers to choose from. Visit your local craft store or go online to see what is available.

Making a Double-Fold Aperture Card

A double-fold card consists of a piece of card folded into three equal sections, with the front section having a window or aperture in it to display your cross stitch embroidery. The front section is stuck to the middle section, thus hiding the back of the embroidery. There are many ready-made double-fold cards available – see Suppliers on page 110 for details of some stockists.

You can also make your own double-fold cards very easily and this will allow you to choose the right card colour to match your embroidery. The instructions below are for a small card but you can easily change the dimensions to suit your embroidery by working with a larger piece of cardstock. Choose a weight of card thick enough to support your stitching, about 160–240gsm. You will need: thick cardstock in a colour of your choice; cutting mat; craft knife and metal ruler; embossing tool and bone folder (optional).

1 Choose a card colour to complement your embroidery and cut a piece 30.5 x 12.7cm (12 x 5in) as shown in Fig 1 (or to the size of your choice). On the wrong side of the card, use a pencil to draw two lines dividing the card into three sections of 10.2cm (4in). Score gently along each line with the back of a craft knife or an embossing tool to make folding easier. Be careful not to cut through the card.

2 In the centre section, mark an aperture slightly bigger than the finished size of the design, leaving a border of about 2.5cm (1in) at the top and bottom and about 1.3cm (½in) at the sides. Place the card on a cutting mat and cut out the aperture with a sharp craft knife and metal ruler, carefully cutting into the corners neatly.

3 Trim the left edge of the first section by 2mm (⅛in) so that it lies flat when folded over to the inside of the card. This will cover the back of the stitching. Fold the left section and then the right section on the scored lines – a bone folder will help you to create a nice, sharp fold. The card is now ready for you to mount your embroidery.

Fig 1 Making a double-fold card

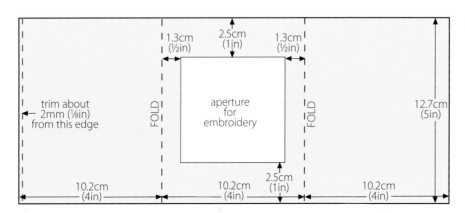

Mounting Embroidery in a Double-Fold Card

1 To mount embroidery in a double-fold card, position the stitching in the window space – the fabric should be at least 2.5cm (1in) larger than the aperture all round. Trim it if necessary.

2 Place strips of double-sided adhesive tape on the card to secure the embroidery (some cards already have this in place). Peel off the tape backing. Alternatively, apply a thin line of glue on the back of the embroidery, about 6mm (¼in) from the edges.

3 Position the embroidery in the window, checking that the design is centred and press down firmly. Fold over the third of the card to cover. This can also be secured with tape for a neater finish. For a personal touch add ribbons, bows, buttons, charms and so on to embellish the card.

Adding Trims and Embellishments

While I chose to keep the finished cards in this book in a clean and simple style, I encourage you to have fun and find what embellishments suit you best. Craft shops, sewing stores and stationery suppliers all have wonderful embellishments that will make each of your cards a reflection of your unique style.

I find it useful to have a special box in my studio to put all the bits and bobs that I may someday use on finished projects. Inside I find ribbons from last year's gifts, an old button from a favourite shirt, or a pretty bead that may one day be just right for a particular card. You will also find that the wide selection of papers, ribbons, markers, toppers, buttons and beads available today will spark your imagination and set your creativity free.

Make sure you have permanent fabric glue or a hot glue gun for attaching your treasures. When choosing ribbons I find that narrow widths work best. Be sure that you use permanent markers if you plan to add some words or tiny drawings to your card mount.

Eastern Promise

Take an exotic journey to the Orient and explore the age-old wisdom of the East. Steeped in tradition, the symbols of Asian culture speak to the many transitions that run through each of our lives. Within the delicate balance of Yin and Yang, our most sincere thoughts can be realized to encourage, soothe and honour those we love, and surround them with gentle messages of harmony, beauty and kindness.

Dancing koi, brilliant flowers and traditional Chinese calligraphy bring best wishes throughout the year. For the man in your life a glorious swirling dragon represents strength and knowledge. A radiant kimono reflects elegance and grace, making a perfect sentiment for the birthday of a special friend. Whether it is a wedding, a new job, or just a note to say 'thinking of you', these cards are just the right way to share your inner spirit.

The elegant cards in this chapter are sure to appeal to many of your friends and family. The beautiful designs can be used in many other ways – see page 27 for suggestions.

Bon Voyage

Historic Blue Willow motifs inspired this card, evoking images of travel to exotic far-off lands. What a lovely way to wish someone a bon voyage before a long journey.

STITCH COUNT 70h x 45w
DESIGN SIZE 12.7 x 8.2cm (5 x 3¼in)

MATERIALS

◆ 25.5 x 20.3cm (10 x 8in) white 14-count Aida
◆ Tapestry needle size 24
◆ DMC stranded cotton (floss) as listed in chart key
◆ Card mount to fit embroidery
◆ Embellishments as desired

1 Prepare for work, marking the centre of the fabric and chart. Start stitching from the centre.

2 Work over one block, using two strands of stranded cotton (floss) for full and three-quarter cross stitches. Work French knots using two strands wound once around the needle. Use one strand for backstitches. Mount in your card, embellishing as desired.

Good Luck

The Japanese kanji character for prosperity is a symbol of good luck so give this card to someone taking a driving test or starting a new job.

STITCH COUNT 70h x 45w
DESIGN SIZE 12.7 x 8.2cm (5 x 3¼in)

MATERIALS

◆ 25.5 x 20.3cm (10 x 8in) white 14-count Aida
◆ Tapestry needle size 24
◆ DMC stranded cotton (floss) as listed in chart key
◆ Kreinik #4 braid 028 citron
◆ Card mount to fit embroidery
◆ Embellishments as desired

Follow step 1 above. Work over one block, using two strands of stranded cotton (floss) for cross stitches. Use one strand for Kreinik #4 Braid cross stitches. Use one strand for backstitches. Mount in your card, embellishing as desired.

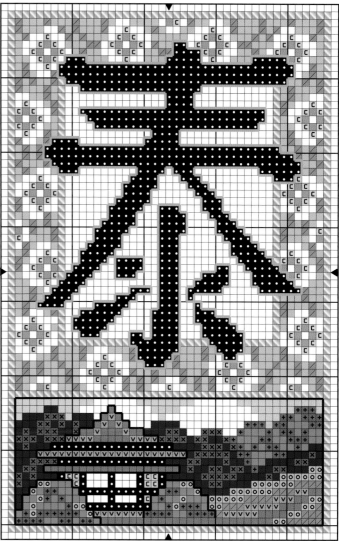

Bon Voyage

DMC stranded cotton

Cross stitch (2 strands)

▨	312	▨	3755
v	334	o	3756
■	336	▨	3841
–	3325	＼	blanc

Backstitch (1 strand)

— 336

French knots (2 strands)

● 336
○ blanc

Good Luck

DMC stranded cotton

Cross stitch (2 strands)

•	310	▨	561
╱	368	▨	832
▨	369	C	834
▨	433	+	3346
v	435	×	3815
▨	471	▨	3840
o	472	▨	Kreinik #4 Braid 028 citron (1 strand)

Backstitch (1 strand)

— 310

▨ Kreinik #4 Braid
028 citron

Birthday Dragon

The lithe figure of a protective Chinese dragon is a symbol of strength and power and makes the perfect birthday card for the man in your life. Gliding amongst the clouds he captures the prized flaming pearl and brings good fortune to your favourite person.

STITCH COUNT 35h x 91w

DESIGN SIZE 6.4 x 16.5cm (2½ x 6½in)

MATERIALS

◆ 19 x 29cm (7½ x 11½in) rumbles of thunder 28-count Jobelan (Polstitches – see Suppliers)

◆ Tapestry needle size 24

◆ DMC stranded cotton (floss) as listed in chart key

◆ Card mount to fit embroidery

◆ Embellishments as desired

1 Prepare for work, marking the centre of the fabric and chart. Start stitching from the centre.

2 Work over two threads, using two strands of stranded cotton (floss) for full and three-quarter cross stitches. Use one strand for backstitches. Mount in your card, embellishing as desired.

Birthday Kimono

The richly coloured silks and exquisite embroidery of the Japanese kimono brought each of these garments to the level of fine art, making them the ultimate symbol of femininity. Make up this wonderful card for a special birthday celebration.

STITCH COUNT 67h x 41w

DESIGN SIZE 12.2 x 7.5cm (4¾ x 3in)

MATERIALS

◆ 24.8 x 20.3cm (9¾ x 8in) white 14-count Aida

◆ Tapestry needle size 24

◆ DMC stranded cotton (floss) as listed in chart key

◆ DMC Satin floss as listed in chart key

◆ Kreinik #4 braid 028 citron

◆ Card mount to fit embroidery

◆ Embellishments as desired

Follow step 1 above. Work over one block using two strands of stranded cotton and satin (floss) for cross stitches. Use one strand for Kreinik #4 braid cross stitches. Use one strand for backstitches. Mount in your card, embellishing as desired.

Celtic Wedding

Share the happiness of a perfect union with the simple, delicate beauty of interlaced Celtic hearts. Glistening gold beads add an extra touch of gleaming sophistication.

STITCH COUNT 43h x 43w
DESIGN SIZE 7.6 x 7.6cm (3 x 3in)

MATERIALS

◆ 20.3 x 20.3cm (8 x 8in) white 28-count Monaco™ (Charles Craft code MO-0236-6750)
◆ Tapestry needle size 24 and a beading needle
◆ DMC stranded cotton (floss) as listed in chart key
◆ Mill Hill Magnifica™ glass beads 10091 gold nugget
◆ Card mount to fit embroidery
◆ Embellishments as desired

1 Prepare for work, marking the centre of the fabric and chart. Start stitching from the centre.

2 Work over two fabric threads, using two strands of stranded cotton (floss) for full and three-quarter cross stitches. Use one strand for Kreinik #4 braid cross stitches. Use one strand for backstitches. Attach beads with a beading needle and matching thread. Mount in your card, embellishing as desired.

Good Wishes

Good wishes abound in the flowering thistle. Protection, strength and deep-rooted ideals will be passed on to the recipient of this symbolic token.

STITCH COUNT 37h x 37w
DESIGN SIZE 6.7 x 6.7cm (2¾ x 2¾in)

MATERIALS

◆ 19.7 x 19.7cm (7¾ x 7¾in) light oatmeal 14-count Fiddler's Cloth™ (Charles Craft code FR-1903-5452)
◆ Tapestry needle size 24
◆ DMC stranded cotton (floss) as listed in chart key
◆ Card mount to fit embroidery
◆ Embellishments as desired

Follow step 1 above. Work over one block, using two strands of stranded cotton (floss) for cross stitches. Use one strand for backstitches. Mount in your card, embellishing as desired.

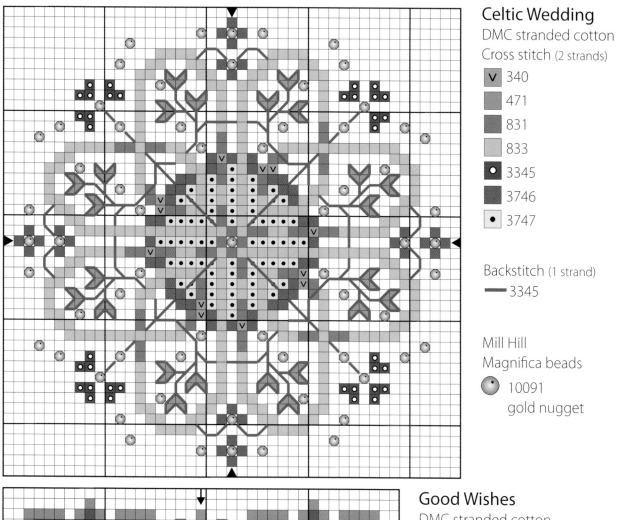

Celtic Wedding

DMC stranded cotton

Cross stitch (2 strands)

V	340
	471
	831
	833
⊙	3345
	3746
•	3747

Backstitch (1 strand)

━━ 3345

Mill Hill
Magnifica beads

⊙ 10091
gold nugget

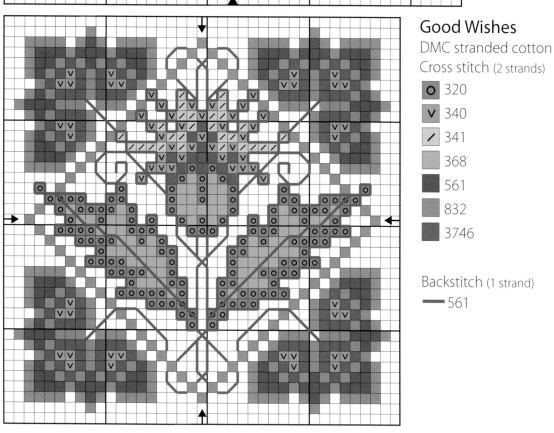

Good Wishes

DMC stranded cotton

Cross stitch (2 strands)

O	320
V	340
∕	341
	368
	561
	832
	3746

Backstitch (1 strand)

━━ 561

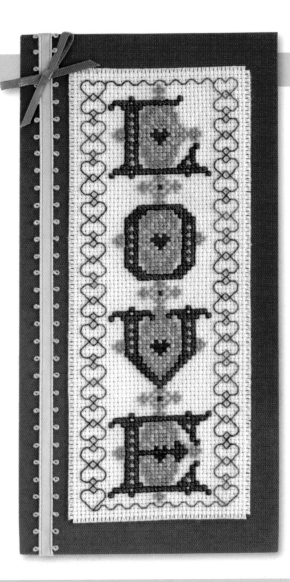

Valentine Love

Illuminated letters in romantically softened tones and a border of intertwining hearts in space-dyed threads show the eternal, enduring quality inherent in the meaning of the word love.

STITCH COUNT 105h x 39w
DESIGN SIZE 16.7 x 6.2cm (6½ x 2½in)

MATERIALS

- ◆ 29 x 19cm (11½ x 7½in) antique white 16-count Aida
- ◆ Tapestry needle size 24
- ◆ DMC stranded cotton (floss) and Color Variations thread as listed in chart key
- ◆ Card mount to fit embroidery
- ◆ Embellishments as desired

1 Prepare for work, marking the centre of the fabric and chart. Start stitching from the centre.

2 Work over one block using two strands of stranded cotton (floss) for cross stitches. Use one strand for backstitches.
Mount in your card, embellishing as desired.

Anniversary Rose

A lovely Celtic rose designed in the Arts and Crafts style is a fitting symbol of love. Create a lasting keepsake and mark the years of a life shared in happiness with this personalized anniversary card. Use the chart on page 109 to change the number and names.

STITCH COUNT 68h x 43w
DESIGN SIZE 12.3 x 7.8cm (5 x 3in)

MATERIALS

- ◆ 25.4 x 20.3cm (10 x 8in) antique white 14-count Aida
- ◆ Tapestry needle size 24
- ◆ DMC stranded cotton (floss) and Color Variations thread as listed in chart key
- ◆ Card mount to fit embroidery
- ◆ Embellishments as desired

Follow step 1 above. Work over one block using two strands of stranded cotton (floss) for cross stitches. Work French knots using two strands wound once around the needle. Use one strand for backstitches. Mount in your card, embellishing as desired.

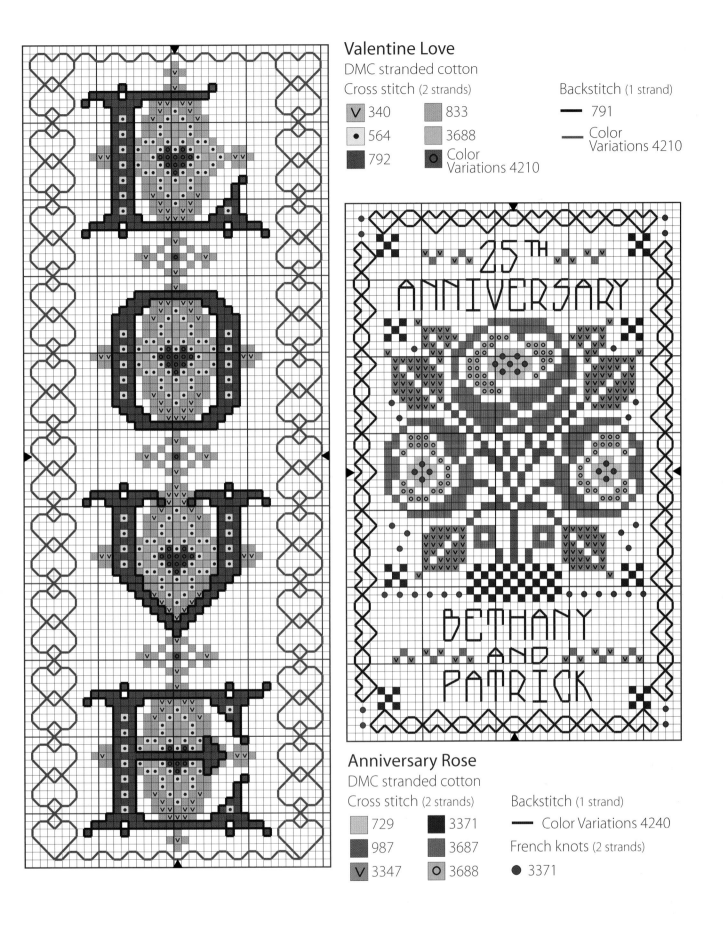

Valentine Love
DMC stranded cotton

Cross stitch (2 strands)

V	340		833
•	564		3688
	792	O	Color Variations 4210

Backstitch (1 strand)
— 791
— Color Variations 4210

Anniversary Rose
DMC stranded cotton

Cross stitch (2 strands)

	729		3371
	987		3687
V	3347	O	3688

Backstitch (1 strand)
— Color Variations 4240

French knots (2 strands)
● 3371

For My Dad

Let Dad know how much he is loved with these stately Celtic lions. Aglow with the warmth of the sun, they bring comforting protection and shine with regal energy.

STITCH COUNT 35h x 53w
DESIGN SIZE 6.4 x 9.6cm (2½ x 3¾in)

MATERIALS

- 19 x 22.2cm (7½ x 8¾in) royal blue 14-count Aida (Zweigart code 3706/540/43)
- Tapestry needle size 24
- DMC stranded cotton (floss) as listed in chart key
- Kreinik #4 braid 150V vintage amber
- Card mount to fit embroidery
- Embellishments as desired

1 Prepare for work, marking the centre of the fabric and chart. Start stitching from the centre.

2 Work over one block using two strands of stranded cotton (floss) for cross stitches. Use one strand for Kreinik #4 braid cross stitches. Work French knots using two strands wound once around the needle. Use one strand for backstitches. Mount in your card, embellishing as desired.

For My Brother

The zoographic animals of Celtic art bring energy and youth to this card made especially for a dear brother. Beautifully detailed knotwork in elfin green metallic threads add extra special sparkle.

STITCH COUNT 43h x 43w
DESIGN SIZE 7.8 x 7.8cm (3 x 3in)

MATERIALS

- 20.3 x 20.3cm (8 x 8in) light oatmeal 14-count Fiddler's Cloth™ (Charles Craft code FR-1903-5452)
- Tapestry needle size 24
- DMC stranded cotton (floss) as listed in chart key
- Kreinik #4 braid 5011 elfin green
- Card mount to fit embroidery
- Embellishments as desired

Follow step 1 above. Work over one block using two strands of stranded cotton (floss) for cross stitches. Use one strand for Kreinik #4 braid cross stitches. Work French knots using two strands wound once around the needle. Use one strand for backstitches. Mount in your card, embellishing as desired.

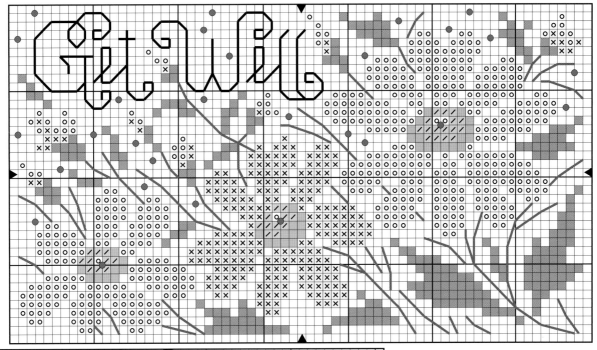

Get Well

DMC stranded cotton

Cross stitch (2 strands)

▨	742	▨	906
⁄	743	⊙	B5200
✕	746		

Backstitch (1 strand)

— 904

— 310

French knots (2 strands)

● 904

Be Strong

DMC stranded cotton

Cross stitch (2 strands)

⁄ 166	● 782	▨ 817	▨ 977	⊙ 3830			
v 434	+ 783	▨ 831	⊙ 3778	▨ Kreinik			
▨ 581	▨ 801	✕ 833	▨ 3826	202HL aztec gold (1 strand)			

Backstitch (1 strand)

— 3371

— Kreinik 202HL aztec gold

With Thanks

In the Victorian language of flowers, bluebells symbolize constancy and humility. Their gently nodding heads send a heartfelt thank you in a most delightful way. The hand-dyed fabric adds to the charm.

STITCH COUNT 35h x 54w
DESIGN SIZE 6.4 x 9.8cm (2½ x 4in)

MATERIALS

- 19 x 23cm (7½ x 9in) rumbles of thunder 28-count Aida (Polstitches – see Suppliers)
- Tapestry needle size 24
- DMC stranded cotton (floss) as listed in chart key
- Card mount to fit embroidery
- Embellishments as desired

1 Prepare for work, marking the centre of the fabric and chart. Start stitching from the centre.

2 Work over two threads using two strands of stranded cotton (floss) for cross stitches. Work French knots using two strands wound once around the needle. Use one strand for backstitches. Mount in your card, embellishing as desired.

Good Luck

With Celtic flair and sparkling gold accents pass along some cheerful good luck wishes with this auspicious four-leafed clover.

STITCH COUNT 49h x 49w
DESIGN SIZE 9 x 9cm (3½ x 3½in)

MATERIALS

- 21.6 x 21.6cm (8½ x 8½in) white Monaco™ 28-count evenweave (Charles Craft code MO-0236-0322-BX)
- Tapestry needle size 24
- DMC stranded cotton (floss) as listed in chart key
- Kreinik #4 braid 028 citron
- Card mount to fit embroidery
- Embellishments as desired

Follow step 1 above. Work over two fabric threads, using two strands of stranded cotton (floss) for full and three-quarter cross stitches. Use one strand for Kreinik #4 braid cross stitches. Use one strand for backstitches. Mount in your card, embellishing as desired.

With Thanks
DMC stranded cotton
Cross stitch (2 strands)
- ● 340
- 341
- 725
- 906
- / 907
- 3746

Backstitch (1 strand)
— 791

French knots (2 strands)
- ● 791

Good Luck
DMC stranded cotton
Cross stitch (2 strands)
- ■ 310
- 905
- ✕ 906
- 907
- Kreinik 028 citron
  (1 strand)

Backstitch (1 strand)
— 310
Kreinik 028 citron

Birthday Wishes

Once on a summer journey to France I remember bicycling down a long hill and suddenly coming upon an endless field of brilliant red poppies – what joy! I've gathered that memory here in a stylish birthday wish.

STITCH COUNT 91h x 35w

DESIGN SIZE 16.5 x 6.4cm (6½ x 2½in)

MATERIALS

- ◆ 29 x 19cm (11½ x 7½in) white 14-count Aida
- ◆ Tapestry needle size 24
- ◆ DMC stranded cotton (floss) as listed in chart key
- ◆ Kreinik #4 braid 028 citron
- ◆ Card mount to fit embroidery
- ◆ Embellishments as desired

1 Prepare for work, marking the centre of the fabric and chart. Start stitching from the centre.

2 Work over one block using two strands of stranded cotton (floss) for cross stitches. Work stranded cotton French knots using two strands wound once around the needle and use one strand for Kreinik French knots. Use one strand for backstitches. Mount in your card, embellishing as desired.

Birthday Wishes

DMC stranded cotton

Cross stitch (2 strands)

● 310	■ 817
■ 317	V 906
● 350	■ 907

Backstitch (1 strand)

— 310
— 904

French knots

● 310 (2 strands)
○ Kreinik 028 (1 strand)

Dear Grandma

DMC stranded cotton

Cross stitch (2 strands)

■ 208	+ 602	743	/ 907			
• 209	603	798	3325			
■ 310	✕ 676	V 799				
601	729	906				

Backstitch (1 strand)

— 310
— 601

French knots (2 strands)

● 310

Dear Grandpa

DMC stranded cotton

Cross stitch (2 strands)

208	603	798	V 907
✕ 209	742	— 800	o blanc
+ 350	• 743	817	
\ 602	744	906	

Backstitch (1 strand)

— 310
— 817

French knots (2 strands)

● 310

Dear Aunt

Always in fashion and the best person ever for spending a fun day wandering the shops, aunties have the ability to make an ordinary day extra special.

STITCH COUNT 27h x 83w
DESIGN SIZE 5 x 15.2cm (2 x 6in)

MATERIALS

- ◆ 18 x 28cm (7 x 11in) white 14-count Aida
- ◆ Tapestry needle size 24
- ◆ DMC stranded cotton (floss) as listed in chart key
- ◆ Card mount to fit embroidery
- ◆ Embellishments as desired

1 Prepare for work, marking the centre of the fabric and chart. Start stitching from the centre.

2 Work over one block using two strands of stranded cotton (floss) for cross stitches. Work French knots using two strands wound once around the needle. Use one strand for backstitches. Mount in your card, embellishing as desired.

Dear Uncle

If your favourite uncle is now the proud owner of a shiny new car or is setting off on a new adventure, here's a fun way to wish him good luck.

STITCH COUNT 27h x 83w
DESIGN SIZE 5 x 15.2cm (2 x 6in)

MATERIALS

- ◆ 18 x 28cm (7 x 11in) white 14-count Aida
- ◆ Tapestry needle size 24
- ◆ DMC stranded cotton (floss) as listed in chart key
- ◆ Card mount to fit embroidery
- ◆ Embellishments as desired

Follow steps 1 and 2 above. Mount in your card, embellishing as desired.

Special Delivery

DMC stranded cotton

Cross stitch (2 strands)

▨	334	C	762
▨	415	▨	907
✕	603	I	951
▨	605	╲	959
▨	743	▨	964
V	744	+	3755
▨	745	╱	blanc

Backstitch (1 strand)

▬▬ 334

▬▬ 603

▬▬ 3799

French knots (2 strands)

● 334

● 743

● 3799

○ blanc

Twice as Nice

DMC stranded cotton

Cross stitch (2 strands)

▨	553	✕	729	╱	964
▨	603	▨	869	▨	Color Variations
V	605	■	938		4050
▨	676	▨	959		

Backstitch (1 strand)

▬▬ 553

▬▬ 603

▬▬ 938

French knots (2 strands)

● 553

● 938

New Arrival

Look who's here! A sweet bundle of joy makes a first appearance, floating in on a colourful balloon with friendly chirping birds along for the ride.

STITCH COUNT 91h x 35w
DESIGN SIZE 16.5 x 6.4cm (6½ x 2½in)

MATERIALS

- 29 x 19cm (11½ x 7½in) antique white 14-count Aida
- Tapestry needle size 24
- DMC stranded cotton (floss) and Color Variations thread as listed in chart key
- Card mount to fit embroidery
- Embellishments as desired

1 Prepare for work, marking the centre of the fabric and chart. Start stitching from the centre.

2 Work over one block using two strands of stranded cotton (floss) for full and three-quarter cross stitches. Work French knots using two strands wound once around the needle. Use one strand for backstitches. Mount in your card, embellishing as desired.

Hello Baby

A brightly smiling sun, a cuddly bunny in his polka dot PJs and a wee duckling along for a ride bring sweetly scented wildflowers to say hello to the newest member of the family.

STITCH COUNT 54h x 35w
DESIGN SIZE 9.8 x 6.4cm (4 x 2½in)

MATERIALS

- 23 x 19cm (9 x 7½in) little boy blue 28-count Lugana (Zweigart code 3270/513/55)
- Tapestry needle size 24
- DMC stranded cotton (floss) and Color Variations thread as listed in chart key
- Card mount to fit embroidery
- Embellishments as desired

Follow step 1 above. Work over two threads using two strands of stranded cotton (floss) for full and three-quarter cross stitches. Work French knots using two strands wound once around the needle. Use one strand for backstitches. Mount in your card, embellishing as desired.

New Arrival

DMC stranded cotton

Cross stitch (2 strands)

- 553
- / 554
- 742
- ∨ 743
- 744
- 799
- 948
- 959
- 962
- • 964
- ⊏ 3325
- × 3716
- ○ blanc
- Color Variations 4050

Backstitch (1 strand)

- —— 938
- —— Color Variations 4050

French knots (2 strands)

- ⚪ 743
- ⚫ 938

Hello Baby

DMC stranded cotton

Cross stitch (2 strands)

- 209
- \ 210
- • 676
- 677
- 729
- 740
- / 742
- 743
- × 744
- 938
- 958
- ∧ 959
- 962
- 964
- + 3716
- 3755
- ○ blanc
- Color Variations 4050

Backstitch (1 strand)

- —— 742
- —— 938
- —— Color Variations 4050

French knots (2 strands)

- ⚫ 938

For Baby

With colourful balloons and twinkling stars the little teddy on this card is ready to join the fun and merriment planned just for baby.

STITCH COUNT 57h x 37w
DESIGN SIZE 10.2 x 6.7cm (4 x 2¾in)

MATERIALS

- ◆ 23 x 20.3cm (9 x 8in) white 14-count Aida
- ◆ Tapestry needle size 24
- ◆ DMC stranded cotton (floss) as listed in chart key
- ◆ Card mount to fit embroidery
- ◆ Embellishments as desired

1 Prepare for work, marking the centre of the fabric and chart. Start stitching from the centre.

2 Work over one block using two strands of stranded cotton (floss) for full and three-quarter cross stitches. Work French knots using two strands wound once around the needle. Use one strand for backstitches. Mount in your card, embellishing as desired.

Baby Gift

With its soft pastel palette, this card would look especially sweet attached to a baby shower gift. You could allow extra fabric and stitch the baby's name below the design using an alphabet from the selection on page 108.

STITCH COUNT 65h x 65w
DESIGN SIZE 9.2 x 9.2cm (3½ x 3½in)

MATERIALS

- ◆ 21.6 x 21.6cm (8½ x 8½in) antique white 18-count Aida
- ◆ Tapestry needle size 24
- ◆ DMC stranded cotton (floss) as listed in chart key
- ◆ Card mount to fit embroidery
- ◆ Embellishments as desired

Follow step 1 above. Work over one block using two strands of stranded cotton (floss) for cross stitches. Use one strand for backstitches. Mount in your card, embellishing as desired.

About the Author

Joan Elliott has been creating needlework designs for nearly 40 years. Her passion for colour and interest in fibres is reflected in all of her work and her distinctive style is well known in the cross stitch world. Joan is also a regular contributor to the cross stitch magazines in both the UK and the US and her kits and books are available worldwide at craft and hobby stores, needlework shops, major booksellers and through online shops and her own website.

Her first book for David and Charles, *A Cross Stitcher's Oriental Odyssey*, was published in 2001 and six more books followed: *Cross Stitch Teddies, Cross Stitch Sentiments and Sayings, Native American Cross Stitch, Cross Stitch Wit & Wisdom, A Woman's World in Cross Stitch* and in 2008 *Bewitching Cross Stitch.*

Joan divides her time between Brooklyn, New York and Vermont, where she is forever inspired by the beauty of the nature that surrounds her. She and her husband feel blessed to have the opportunity to share the many joys and experiences that both city and country life have to offer.

Acknowledgments

Much love and many thanks go to the talented stitchers that have once again amazed me with their skill and artistry. This book would not have been possible without your many dedicated hours of work on these projects. It is in friendship and joy that I write your names here: Lisa Rabon, Bev Ritter, Judi Trochimiak, MaryAnn Stephens, Lori West, Charlie Rosenberger, Robyn Purta, Sharon Schutjer, Debbie Fitzgerald, Lynda Moss, Brandy Merrell and Maria Massa.

To Cheryl Brown, my original commissioning editor, I send my love. Your enthusiasm and inspiration is still with me and I will be forever grateful for our years of wonderfully creative collaboration and for the many doors you have opened for me. You are one of a kind!

To Ali Myer and Jennifer Fox-Proverbs, I send thanks for seeing this project through to completion. Thanks to Kim Sayer and Karl Adamson for the excellent photography and to designer Victoria Marks for her lovely book design.

For my editor Lin Clements, may this book be one huge thank you card for everything. Through this trying year for my family, your voice has supported, comforted and cheered me. It truly has been a special gift. I know your confident expertise has made this book the best it can be.

Index